Meditations for Financial Freedom

VOLUME 3

DeForest B. Soaries, Jr.

CORPORATE COMMUNITY CONNECTIONS, INC.

CORPORATE COMMUNITY CONNECTIONS, INC.

Published by Corporate Community Connections, Inc. / Faith in Action Publishing

Copyright © 2021 DeForest B. Soaries, Jr. All rights reserved.

Book Packaging: Earl Cox & Associates Worldwide

ISBN 13: 978-1-7356124-1-6
LCNN: 2016933840

Cataloging in Publication Data

Names:	Soaries, DeForest B., author.
Title:	Meditations for financial freedom; v.3 / DeForest B. Soaries, Jr.
Description:	First edition. I Monmouth Junction, NJ : Corporate Community Connections, Inc., [2021] I Series: Meditations for financial freedom ; v. 3
Identifiers:	ISBN: 978-1-7356124-1-6 I 978-1-7356124-2-3 (ebook)
Subjects:	LCSH: Finance, Personal--Religious aspects--Christianity. I Saving and investment--Religious aspects--Christianity. I Retirement--Planning--Religious aspects--Christianity. I Entrepreneurship--Religious aspects--Christianity. I Consumer credit--Religious aspects--Christianity. I BISAC: RELIGION / Biblical Meditations / General. I RELIGION / Biblical Criticism & Interpretation / General. I BUSINESS & ECONOMICS / Personal Finance / General.

Classification: LCC: HG179 .S63 2016 I DDC: 332.024--dc23

Printed in the United States of America

First Edition: 2021

All scripture quotations, unless otherwise indicated, are taken from the Holy Bible, *New International Version*®, NIV®. Copyright © 1973, 1978, 1984 by Biblica, IncTM. All rights reserved worldwide.

TABLE OF CONTENTS

INTRODUCTION

Welcome to *Meditations for Financial Freedom Volume 3*!

In a rapidly changing world with unprecedented challenges, it is good to know that there is certainty to be found in the Word of God. Although the Bible is not always easy to understand, the principles contained in Biblical stories can guide and inspire us in our daily sojourn. I have found great comfort and strength in becoming more and more familiar with the Bible and allowing its messages to function as my primary source of light and hope.

I am especially grateful for the way my study of the Bible has helped shape my relationship with money. I spent so many years dodging bill collectors, paying late fees for delinquent bills, and penalties for insufficient funds in my bank account. I can't calculate the thousands of dollars I must have wasted in these areas of my financial life.

I waited longer than I am willing to admit to take responsibility for my financial affairs. No one could tell by looking at me that I was living in poverty. I fooled many because I dressed in nice clothes and drove nice cars. I was living a lie.

The death of my paternal grandmother was a catalytic moment for me. She had no formal education beyond grade school and worked as a seamstress in the garment district of New York. Her husband had had a stroke and could not work to support the family.

As a black woman in New York living through the Great Depression and facing racial discrimination, Carrie L. Soaries could have justifiably depended on public assistance. However, my grandmother not only worked her vocation to provide for her six children and disabled husband, but also acquired a license to sell real estate.

By the time she died, she owned three houses that were fully paid for, one of which is where I was born in Brooklyn, New York. She also bequeathed one of the three houses to my uncle and I when she died, and it became the first real estate I ever owned.

That inheritance did two things for me: First, it got me started on accruing real estate assets. Second, it made me aware of the fact that I was living a financially reckless life. I knew I needed to change in order to leave an inheritance for my own children.

I knew that my grandmother read the Bible every morning. It became clear to me that her wisdom and her strategies had come directly from her daily meditations. I have gladly embraced the habit that I observed in my grandmother, and I have also found great joy in sharing the results of my meditations with others.

This volume of *Meditations* draws on highlights from the books of 1 Samuel and 2 Samuel. I hope these thoughts and prayers will support your own efforts to maintain faith and focus as you allow God to bless you and use you to bless others.

DeForest B. Soaries, Jr.

FAMILY

Verse

"Whenever the day came for Elkanah to sacrifice,
he would give portions of the meat to his wife
Peninnah and to all her sons and daughters."
1 Samuel 1:4 NIV

Thought

I have been a pastor for almost forty-five years. As important as it has been to recruit and motivate church members to serve God, I have also challenged my church members and staff to make sure they make the needs of their families their priority. No one should allow any activity or commitment -even religion or religious practice- to supersede providing for their families. That is what Elkanah was careful to do.

Elkanah was a priest. It was the job of the priest to offer animal sacrifices to God on behalf of his community. These sacrifices represented a kind of apology to God for the mistakes people made in their lives. These sacrifices required priests to kill very valuable animals; animals that were owned by the people in the community; animals that had no blemish, disease, or flaw.

It is safe to assume that some people refused to kill their best animals for religious purposes. They did not believe in God that much. Others were probably so devoted to God that they offered their sacrifices and kept nothing for themselves or their families. While that may have made them feel noble and perhaps righteous, that actually meant they were using religion as an excuse to neglect their families. This priest, Elkanah, decided to strike a balance. He was able to fulfill his religious obligation as a priest by offering a sacrifice *and* fulfill his obligations as a provider by giving portions of the meat to his wife and children.

Our families deserve to be our priority. I have tried to remain aware that my church can always get another pastor, but my children can never get another father. I have missed church services to attend my sons' basketball games and I never missed a parent/teacher conference while they were students in school. I also made it a priority to have everyone's needs included in our family budget.

If we don't care for our families, no one else will. Caring for our families means maintaining a balance between our worthy pursuits and activities, as well as our families' needs and desires.

Prayer

"God, help me to never lose focus of my family and our needs. Amen."

Decision

Today I have decided to: _____

_____

_____

_____

_____

2 CHILDREN

Verse

"After he was weaned, she [Hannah] took the boy [Samuel] with her, young as he was, along with a three-year-old bull, an ephah of flour and a skin of wine, and brought him to the house of the Lord at Shiloh." 1 Samuel 1:24 NIV

Thought

Many people tell me that when they were children, the only conversation they had with their parents about money was when they would ask for something and their parents told them that they could not afford it. One of the lasting impressions my dad left with me is the paperwork he left in his safe deposit box when he died. The contents of that box were an indication of how thorough and organized he was concerning his personal business.

Dad died at forty-seven years old. A week prior to his death, my dad took me to the bank to review the papers that related to his personal business. This was both a humbling and frightening experience as a twenty-three-year-old. I was honored that he considered me capable of handling family business should something happen to him. After his passing, I was grateful that was not the first time my father discussed money with me. My parents were like Elkanah and Hannah; they exposed me to family business and our financial practices at a young age.

My dad would show me his bill paying practices; including what he did when he didn't have the money to pay certain bills. The most important instruction I received as a child was the practice of tithing. In my book, *Say Yes to No Debt*, I describe my tithing practice as having begun as a child. When I received a gift or any other form of financial increase, I was taught to give 10% to God as my tithe offering. When my parents took me to church, as Hannah took Samuel, I would place my offering into the plate just as my mother would place hers. This was instruction by example.

Children become consumers at a very early age. By the time we take them with us to the supermarket they have already been exposed to advertising and know what cereal and other products they prefer; and they are certainly not shy about sharing that information with their parents!

We should be intentional and aggressive about teaching our children about finances in general, and specifically family finances. They should be exposed to our income and expenses with an emphasis on the expenses that relate to them. As soon as he had been weaned from his mother's breast, Samuel went to church with his mother and saw her give her offering. That impression stayed with him all of his life, as it did with my parents and I. We must not forsake the need to teach our children at an early age and our teaching *must* include lessons about money.

Samuel became a great prophet, and his parents had a lot to do with that. Who our children become will have a lot to do with what we teach them long before they ever attend school.

Prayer

"God, help me to instruct my children about your principles regarding money. Amen."

Decision

Today I have decided to: _____

_____

_____

_____

_____

3 POVERTY

Verse

*"He raises the poor from the dust and lifts the
needy from the ash heap; he seats them with
princes and has them inherit a throne of honor.
'For the foundations of the earth are the Lord's;
on them he has set the world.'"*
1 Samuel 2:8 NIV

Thought

These words were a part of Hannah's prayer to God. The
entire prayer is found in 1 Samuel 2:1-10. The prayer was a
thanksgiving prayer combined with a testimony. God had
elevated Hannah from a state of barrenness to a position
of spiritual and physical victory. Her prayer not only
thanks God for what he has done, but it acknowledges
that God's blessing for her was just a small sample of
what God does for the downtrodden. She knew that God
was capable of many blessings. Hannah was incapable of
getting pregnant and bearing a child, but God changed
her condition. Hannah could testify that not only could
God make the barren bear children, but that he could
also do other great deeds; including bring people out of
poverty. That is really amazing, and to that I say, Amen!

Poverty is a curse. It is heartbreaking to see so much wealth in the hands of so few people and so much poverty engulfing the lives of so many others. I have spent time living with people that survive on just a few dollars a week. I know others that spend more money for one dinner in a fancy restaurant than many earn in a year. Although poverty is fundamentally an economic reality, there is a spiritual component to getting out of poverty. I say that because changing any human circumstance begins with the belief of the person seeking change.

I am aware that there are systems and conditions that make it nearly impossible for certain people to rise out of poverty. Therefore, there is never a guarantee that poverty can be ended with just faith, or by a belief system alone. What is true, however, is when someone does make it out of poverty, it always starts with a change in what the person believes is true and possible.

Until I believed that I could live without getting calls from bill collectors, writing overdrawn checks and accruing mountains of debt, my life stayed the same. When I changed my thinking and added the belief that God would give me the help I needed, then my life started moving in a different direction. Hannah's belief that God could do many great things was based on her experience that God had done *one* great thing for her. If we can identify one great deed God has done in our lives, we will remember that if God did that one great deed, he can do any great deed, including helping someone rise above poverty.

Prayer

"God, give me compassion for the poor and use me to give hope and help to someone in need. Amen."

Decision

Today I have decided to: _____

_____

_____

_____

_____

4 CORRUPTION

Verse

*"I will raise up for myself a faithful priest, who will
do according to what is in my heart and mind.
I will firmly establish his priestly house, and they
will minister before my anointed one always.
Then everyone left in your family line will come
and bow down before him for a piece of silver
and a loaf of bread and plead, 'Appoint me to
some priestly office so I can have food to eat.'"*
1 Samuel 2:35-36 NIV

Thought

Leadership is a gift from God. God saw it fit to plant into
the human spirit the appointment for certain people to
lead others. It is a necessary tool for the progress of human
nature. From people who are elected to hold public offices
to leaders of religious organizations, they all inherit this
intangible but present willingness of humans to invest
hope and trust in them. Benefits are bestowed on such
people that are held in high esteem by others. Whether
one is the head of a global enterprise or a local community
associate, there is a level of esteem that translates into

tangible and intangible benefits that leaders enjoy. That makes a leadership position a privilege that should be accepted with humility, and should be taken seriously.

Hophni and Phineas were two young men who were in a position of status and enjoyed many benefits due to the family in which they belonged. They were the sons of Eli; a highly esteemed priest. In this chapter, Hophni and Phineas were introduced as scoundrels; "Eli's sons were scoundrels; they had no regard for the Lord" (1 Samuel 2:12). How tragic that the man that is probably the most respected person in the community has sons that have become the least respected. This description resulted from their own behavior. They chose to misuse their father's respectability to take advantage of the very people that their father led. They were corrupt.

Their corruption may have seemed minor, but what was a small human matter was a big deal for God. With God there is no such thing as a small sin or a big sin. My dad used to always say, "To God, sin *is* sin!"

We must be careful to avoid cutting corners and embracing a tolerance for committing small sins in order to propel financially. Cheating on our income taxes, breaking our promises, accepting more than we are due, and other small sins are not only significant to God, but they can easily turn into larger infractions. I know an attorney that borrowed a few dollars from one of his clients' escrow accounts. That small loan turned into a million-dollar scandal. The attorney was disbarred and lost everything he had because of something that started off small and grew into a major problem.

The best definition of integrity I ever heard was this: "Integrity is when you will do what's right even if there is no possible chance of ever being caught doing what is wrong." That makes integrity the preventive cure for corruption.

Prayer

"God, give me integrity. Amen."

Decision

Today I have decided to: _____

_____

_____

_____

_____

5 EBENEZER

Verse

"Then Samuel took a stone and set it up between Mizpah and Shen. He named it Ebenezer, saying, 'Thus far the Lord has helped us.'"
1 Samuel 7:12 NIV

Thought

I have always been fascinated by the names that people use to identify their churches. Martin Luther King, Jr. grew up in a church that was in a segregated section of Atlanta, Georgia. When the church was organized by thirteen Black people in 1886, they named it Ebenezer Baptist Church. There is no doubt that the name was inspired from the name of the stone raised by Samuel to commemorate a victory over the Philistines at Mizpah. I am also certain that the people that organized the church were inspired by the victory of their emancipation from slavery. They wanted the very name of their church to serve as a reminder that while conditions for their people were not desirable, God still had helped them, thus far.

Whenever we focus on things we plan to do, places we plan to go and things we want to accomplish, there exists an assumption that we desire more and that life should be a perpetual process of attaining more; more knowledge, more happiness, more exposure, more wisdom, and certainly more assets. If in three years I find myself with the same level of savings, same amount of debt, same amount of assets, unless I experienced an unavoidable illness or tragedy, I will consider myself as having failed. I want consistent growth and progress.

However, I have learned that between my right now and my not yet, I should always remember how I arrived where I am. Thus far suggests that God has been with me and that God will continue to be with me. Sometimes the presence of God is so obvious. Divine intervention is when things happen that have no logical explanation except God. Like the recovery of the Ark of the Covenant from the Philistines that only God could have orchestrated. Sometimes, God intentionally steps in by getting us a job offer for a position in which we were not qualified or by sparing us from disaster. For example, my neighbor missed his train to work at the World Trade Center on September 11, 2001 and was therefore not killed in that terrorist attack!

The more we recognize the help that God has given, the more likely it is that we will settle into the reality that God will continue being the God that helps us. Robert

Robinson put it like this in the second verse of his great hymn, *Come Thou Fount of Every Blessing*:

> *"Here I raise my Ebenezer,*
> *Hither by Thy help I've come;*
> *And I hope, by Thy good pleasure,*
> *Safely to arrive at home."*

This perspective defies the concept of the self-made man or the self-made woman. There *must* be a God somewhere aiding along the way.

Prayer

"God, may I never forget that you are my Ebenezer. Amen."

Decision

Today I have decided to: _____

_____

_____

_____

_____

NEEDS

Verse

"Then we will be like all the other nations, with a king to lead us and to go out before us and fight our battles." 1 Samuel 8:20 NIV

Thought

When I was a kid, there were three types of athletic shoes that were considered appropriate when playing basketball. In my state, New Jersey, the brand of choice was Chuck Taylor Converse All Stars. In New York City, where I learned to play basketball, the brand of choice was PRO-Keds. Then there were what we called, no-brand sneakers – meaning all other brands. Since my dad was raised in Brooklyn and was a passionate basketball fan and player, I was certain that I would either wear Chuck Taylor's or PRO-Keds. I could not have been more mistaken. My father decided that a no-brand sneaker was more reasonable in cost compared to the brand-named sneakers. He made sure that he stuck to his budget, even if that meant that I would face embarrassment for not having what everyone else was wearing.

Wanting what other people have can eat away at us the same way termites can destroy the foundation of a house. I wanted those sneakers, and no one could change my mind about them. There was absolutely no evidence that the expensive sneakers increased a players' performance; they were simply the style.

Israel wanted a king because that is what other nations had. Even though no other nation had experienced the miracles Israel had, they still wanted what was common among their neighbors. Israel was making a serious mistake – the same mistake that we sometimes make regarding our finances. They were preoccupied with other people!

We sometimes spend money to have what other people have. Unfortunately, too often those purchases exceed the lifestyle we can afford. The real question is whether or not we needed what we purchased or whether we simply wanted them.

One of the most important exercises we can do is to make a list of your wants and your needs, and then compare the two. In my book, *dfree® Lifestyle: 12 Steps to Financial Freedom*, there is a chart to facilitate such an exercise. I have been so surprised to see how many people have never made such a list. If we have never distinguished between *wants* and *needs*, we may never achieve financial freedom because our spending for wants can overtake our spending for needs.

God has promised to provide all of our needs. But if we don't know the difference, we won't know when God has kept his promise.

Israel failed to understand that in God, they had the only king they needed.

Prayer

"God, help me to decipher between my wants and my needs. Amen."

Decision

Today I have decided to: _____

_____

_____

_____

_____

DAY
7   THANKS

Verse

"So all the people went to Gilgal and made Saul king in the presence of the Lord. There they sacrificed fellowship offerings before the Lord, and Saul and all the Israelites held a great celebration." 1 Samuel 11:15 NIV

Thought

Although my parents did not buy me all of the things that I wanted, I was raised in a relatively comfortable, middle income home. Of course, my parents worked very hard to make that possible. Nevertheless, we were fortunate enough to never know anything about collecting unemployment checks or depending upon public assistance to meet our daily needs. We never took extravagant vacations, but, when we did take summer trips to a small, black owned lodge in New York, we travelled in the family car. We never took a family flight to a destination, but we owned a television and a car, and *that* made us middle class.

Up until college, I had taken my upbringing for granted. It wasn't until college that I met students that came from families that survived on government assistance programs and whose tuition was being paid by government funds, that I began to realize that everyone that looked like me wasn't fortunate enough to grow up like me. After I became a minister, I travelled to Jamaica and The West Indies; it was these places that helped me understand the meaning of real poverty. Coming face-to-face with people that lived with no running water, no electricity, and no pavement on their streets, made me realize how I had taken my lifestyle for granted and had never properly thanked anyone, including God, for all of my many blessings.

I should have taken my direction from the Israelites who were blessed to receive something they really didn't need – a king. In response, as a part of the ceremony that made Saul King of Israel, they thanked God by making sacrifices to him. They knew that simply saying, "Thanks," was not enough. A sacrifice is more than a mere gift. A sacrifice is something that one has the right to keep and use for themselves, but instead they offer it as an expression of thanks to someone else.

When we realize that millions of people are literally starving at this very moment, it should not depart from us to offer our thanks in the form of offerings and sacrifice for what God has done in our lives. Our willingness to give sacrificial offerings should not be investments in the return that we want from God. Rather, our offerings should simply be expressions of thanks for what God has already done for us.

Prayer

"God, give me a grateful spirit that results in giving. Amen."

Decision

Today I have decided to: _____

_____

_____

_____

_____

LONGEVITY

Verse

"Saul was thirty years old when he became king, and he reigned over Israel forty-two years."
1 Samuel 13:1 NIV

Thought

My pastor served our church for fifty-four years. That is an unimaginable feat; to be doing one job for more than half a century. That is an admirable accomplishment. What dedication, determination, and imagination one must have to remain engaged in the same task for that length of time.

Longevity has its ups and downs. King Saul certainly learned that during his forty-two-year tenure as the leader of his nation. As the years of Saul's leadership unfolded, he had bouts of jealousy, insecurity and depression. One time, he actually sought help from the worst possible source of guidance and encouragement – Saul went to see a witch!

I have learned many things from my pastor. One thing he has taught me has helped me understand the potential for sustaining longevity. One can avoid being bored in a position when one has healthy outlets that protect him from being consumed by that one job or position. One of Saul's mistakes was that his job was his life. He did ask young David to play music for him when he became overwhelmed, but clearly that was not enough. My pastor was involved in civic and political activities outside of his pastoral position. Not only did these outlets diversify his associations, but they also provided him with information and relationships that he could use to help the members of the church. He not only was a leader in the church but also in government, and in the community. He utilized his pastoral skills to make an impact outside of the church and he used his exposure to remain relevant to the members that listened to his weekly sermons. He never got bored.

I have tried to practice what I learned from my pastor. During my thirty years as Senior Pastor of First Baptist Church of Lincoln Gardens, I have been active in community, corporate and governmental affairs. These involvements have allowed me to be excited and engaged in various things in order to maintain longevity; much more than I would have, had my entire life been consumed by my job.

It is much easier to remain motivated, refreshed, vibrant and relevant when maintaining a long-term position if one does not allow that one role to take over one's entire life. God has blessed us with one-hundred and eighty-six hours every week. There is ample time to spend a few of those hours engaged in healthy outlets that add meaning and value to life.

Prayer

"Dear God, help me diversify my activities and avoid being consumed by my job. Amen."

Decision

Today I have decided to: _____

_____

_____

_____

_____

9 DUTY

Verse

"But Samuel replied: 'Does the Lord delight in burnt offerings and sacrifices as much as in obeying the Lord? To obey is better than sacrifice, and to heed is better than the fat of rams.'"
1 Samuel 15:22NIV

Thought

Can you imagine someone robbing a bank and then claiming that they did so in order to help their church buy a new bus? As preposterous as this sounds, there are people that justify committing crimes because of their intention to be noble with the proceeds. There is a former government official in jail right now because he took a bribe from a real estate developer that wanted to do business in his city. When asked why he took the bribe, the official said that he took the money to help a little league baseball team. I am sure the children on that team would have loved receiving the politician's donation, but the intention to donate did not absolve the official of the crime that he committed to secure the funds. The average person understands this perfectly. However, we seem to be a bit fuzzy when it involves violating *Divine Laws*.

When it comes to God's laws, there is no police department that holds us accountable for breaking them. God's laws are meant to be upheld, however, we become very comfortable in breaking God's laws when we see fit. We are very comfortable in accepting and respecting the laws that benefit us, but we struggle to uphold the laws that benefit God and his people.

For instance, we don't mind the law of gravity. Without gravity we would not be able to enjoy life as we know it. The law of gravity is just one component of how God created and ordered the earth. It is a law that we benefit from, but have no choice other than to obey it. It is not optional.

There are also laws and standards that apply to finances. The Bible is full of principles, instructions, rules and laws that address finances. In ancient Israel, farmers were required to leave one tenth of their harvest to provide gleaning opportunities for poor people. That was the rule, the law, the standard. God still requires that we use one tenth of our income as the standard for supporting God's work through God's churches; but most of us consider that standard as being optional.

We justify it by pointing to all of the good things that we do for our families and others. That is exactly what Saul did. He brought offerings to be sacrificed, but the offerings came from animals that God told him to destroy. He disobeyed God, but wanted to justify his disobedience by offering a portion of his ill-gotten gain to the religious service. The prophet Samuel responded by telling Saul that doing something religious did not please God – *obedience to God's command is what pleases God*!

When I was a child, children didn't question their parents. If I would ever conjure the courage to ask my father why I had to do something that he had told me to do, his answer would be, "because I said so." No explanation offered; his words had absolute authority.

We must obey God's laws in the same way. *He* has absolute authority. Financial freedom requires that we obey the rules made by God. When we put God first and give God the *first* one tenth of what we earn, we have established a pattern of obedience that generates immeasurable benefits in our lives. It is better to obey God than to be generous with what we should have given to God.

Prayer

"God, give me the faith and the courage to obey you in my giving. Amen."

Decision

Today I have decided to: _____
_____
_____
_____
_____

APPEARANCE

Verse

"But the Lord said to Samuel, 'Do not consider his appearance or his height, for I have rejected him. The Lord does not look at the things people look at. People look at the outward appearance, but the Lord looks at the heart.'" 1 Samuel 16:7 NIV

Thought

We've all heard the old adage, "You can't judge a book by its cover." However, it is almost impossible to avoid doing that.

I was once trying to close the largest transaction of my life. I had tens of thousands of personal dollars invested that I would never recoup if the transaction did not close by a certain date. After exhausting all of my available resources and meeting with every conceivable connection to try and find a solution, I was referred to someone that I did not know but had a reputation for getting the job done. The meeting was set to occur at an airport hotel, and I arrived about an hour early. The man that I was there to meet arrived late. That was the first of many unsettling aspects from our first meeting. When he did arrive, he was wearing a suit that looked as if he had worn it to bed; it was wrinkled, well-worn and deserving of a replacement. To add to his disheveled appearance, his hair had not seen a barber and he was in desperate need of a shave. His shoes were unpolished and what we used to call, run over. After he introduced himself, he fumbled through the stack of papers he brought that included descriptions of transactions that he had previously closed before finding the few that he wanted to show me. This was supposed to be my knight in shining armor? He looked like my long-lost relative coming to borrow money from me.

I almost broke down in tears. By looking at him, I was convinced that he wouldn't be able to help me and I would lose out on my investment. But in the end, he was in fact the person that I needed and had succeeded with handling the transaction. My opinions of people have now become shaped by performance rather than appearance.

I will never recommend that anyone arrive late for a meeting, and when they do arrive, look like they have slept in their clothes; but I have learned to save my assessments of people until I understand what they can do versus how they look. I could have failed with a big project had I not learned that lesson.

The future King of Israel, David, did not look like a king. His own father did not see him as a potential king. However, despite his looks, David had been selected by

God to be anointed by the prophet Samuel, rather than any of his brothers that *looked* the part.

As the next generation becomes the dominant age group in the workplace, we will find that they don't dress the way previous generations dressed and don't have the same traditional assumptions about work that their predecessors had. However, their appearances should not determine what opportunities they are given; they are the architects of our future. And just as I have learned, when you judge a book by its cover, they just might surprise you.

Prayer

"God, help me to look beyond the way people appear. Amen."

Decision

Today I have decided to: _____

_____

_____

_____

_____

BARRIERS

Verse

"So David triumphed over the Philistine with a sling and a stone; without a sword in his hand he struck down the Philistine and killed him."
1 Samuel 17:50 NIV

Thought

Few Bible stories are as well-known as this one, where a little shepherd boy named David, encounters a giant warrior named Goliath. All soldiers were intimidated by Goliath, but David did not see him as an insurmountable obstacle. I once heard a preacher say that while the soldiers said that Goliath was too big to kill, David was saying that Goliath was too big to miss!

There are always barriers that have the potential to stop our progress. Some barriers are racial; some are economic; some are political; some are circumstantial. When I was 19-years-old, I made a mistake that resulted in me being arrested. For a long time, I allowed this mistake to be a barrier in my pursuit of opportunity. I believed that I would never be able to get a good job or do anything meaningful because I had an arrest on my record. Despite that blemish, I have been afforded great jobs and opportunities. Thanks be to God!

I have learned to name all of my barriers Goliath – because in the end, Goliath was destroyed. If we see our Goliath's such as David did (too big to miss), we can destroy the barriers that seek to stop us.

David understood that Goliath was not *all* powerful. We sometimes feel as if our set-backs have more power than they do. As long as we are still breathing, we have the ability to overcome our barriers. It helps when we remember that our current barrier is not our first barrier; and if our last barrier did not destroy us, this one will not either. David's people had experienced many victories in their past and he realized that they had defeated enemies and obstacles more formidable than Goliath. He refused to give Goliath more credit than he was due. God was greater than Goliath. God *is* greater than your Goliath!

Another thing we can learn from David is to ignore the naysayers. David's own brother tried to discourage him from addressing Goliath; but David was committed to his purpose and would not listen to his older brother. Sometimes our dreams and our destinies are aborted because we listen to the voices of others who can't see what we see. Be careful to choose those with whom you share your dream. Be prepared to ignore the discouraging advice you receive from people that may have good intentions, but have underestimated your potential. It is better to fail knowing that you tried your best, than to give up before seeing how far you can go. David would have never defeated Goliath if he had doubted himself and allowed his brother to have the last word.

Finally, David used his own strategy and not the king's. When offered the king's sword and armor, David responded by stating that he trusted God to give him victory using his own tools. He used a slingshot and a stone instead of a sword and a spear. If we always remember to be ourselves and to depend on God's power, nothing can stop us from getting past our barriers.

Prayer

"God, help me be unintimidated by any barrier placed in my path. Amen."

Decision

Today I have decided to: _____

_____

_____

_____

_____

12 JEALOUSY

Verse

"Saul was very angry; this refrain displeased him greatly. 'They have credited David with tens of thousands,' he thought, 'but me with only thousands. What more can he get but the kingdom?' And from that time on Saul kept a close eye on David." 1 Samuel 18:8-9 NIV

Thought

I have been asked to assist people in every conceivable category of life. I have been asked to help people with raising their children; I have been invited to help people rescue failing businesses; I have been requested to give advice to government leaders on public policies; I have been sought after by clergy concerning church matters; I even helped entertainers with strategies related to their careers; and I have been called upon to pray for the sick and counsel those who were in distress. But I have never been asked to counsel or advise someone that needed help or prayer because they were overcome by jealousy.

Jealousy does not seem to be a condition that we readily admit that we have. Although it is not unusual for people to describe others as having signs of being jealous of someone, rarely, if ever, do people self-diagnose and admit that they are jealous of others.

Saul was king and David worked for him. Saul was older than David and more accomplished in his life than David. Yet Saul was jealous of David. People praised David for having done something that Saul had not done and Saul was so jealous that he became distracted by David and lost focus on himself and his mission.

There is nothing wrong with having role models and mentors. In fact, it is advisable to identify a few people from whom you can emulate and extract lessons. I have learned so much about leading a large congregation from my pastor, Rev. Dr. Samuel Howard Woodson, Jr.; I learned so much about preaching, speaking and writing from my mentor, Rev. Dr. Samuel DeWitt Proctor; and I learned so much about Biblical scholarship under the instruction of my academic mentor and advisor, Rev. Dr. Byron Shafer. But as much as I admire these three men, I cannot be any one of them.

That is what jealousy involves – wishing we were someone else and even trying to become them. Jealousy is wanting what someone else has and feeling inferior because we don't have it. Jealousy eats away at our self-esteem, our sense of confidence and our perspective concerning our purpose. Jealousy shows up in our behavior often disguised as constructive criticism or even legitimate critique. There are people jealous of you that you think are your friends, but they really resent your success, your intelligence, your discipline, your good looks, your integrity, your other friendships and even your goals.

If you find yourself paying more attention to others than to yourself, you may be watering seeds of jealousy. No one may know besides you, but if you find yourself really hating hearing good news about someone else – or resenting it when someone achieves something significant – go ahead and admit that you are jealous. Then turn your jealousy into positive energy and do what you need to do to achieve what you have the potential to achieve.

If you read Saul's background, you will notice that he had some very impressive credentials. However, his jealousy caused him to forget about his own attributes and strengths, and focus on David's. There it is – the solution for jealousy. When we identify our own strengths, our own gifts, our own potential, we become so busy building our own paths and pursuing our own dreams that we don't have time to do what Saul did – *"keep a close eye on David."* Instead, let us focus on our own successes and futures, so that we can genuinely celebrate the successes of others while we realize and work on our own.

Prayer

"God, please remove all jealousy from my being. Amen."

Decision

Today I have decided to: _____

_____

_____

_____

_____

LOYALTY

Verse

*"Saul told his son Jonathan and all the
attendants to kill David. But Jonathan had taken
a great liking to David and warned him, 'My
father Saul is looking for a chance to kill you.
Be on your guard tomorrow morning; go into
hiding and stay there. I will go out and stand
with my father in the field where you are. I'll
speak to him about you and will tell you what I
find out.'"* 1 Samuel 19:1-3 NIV

Thought

Throughout my career, I have always advocated for
small, minority owned businesses in an effort to promote
economic opportunity and racial uplift. This has always
been a passion of mine. Small businesses create more jobs
every year than major corporations. I understand that
in order for racial wealth gaps to close, particularly for
Black Americans, business development and expansion
is a must. Therefore, I am unapologetically supportive of
minority and women owned businesses and I always will

be. This belief led to a misunderstanding and resulted in the loss of a friend.

My friend loved that I carried this belief. What made him change his mind about me was when he learned I hired someone to handle a business matter for me that was not a minority. Additionally, my friend's business did the exact work that I hired the other person to do. The last time we met, he refused to shake my hand, and he died believing that I was a complete hypocrite.

What my former friend never gave me a chance to explain was that the person that I hired helped me resolve a previous transaction that was very complicated. In fact, the person was not only helpful, but put their money into the transaction. That transaction wouldn't have been possible if he had not made that sacrifice because I was completely out of funds. As a result of that person's support and investment in my business, I promised him that I would repay him by allowing his company to handle my next transaction. It was paramount for me to keep my word and to be loyal to someone who had been kind to me. In that instance, my loyalty to keep my word was more important.

Jonathan's father told him to kill David; but Jonathan was David's friend and had promised David that they would remain friends for life. For Jonathan, his vow to David was more important than his father's orders. He was loyal to David. He had no legal obligation to David any more than I had with the person who helped me. But as Jesus taught us, he treated David in the manner that he would have wanted to be treated. When Jonathan warned and helped David, he demonstrated the belief that loyalty is thicker than blood.

In life, loyalty should beget loyalty. I have found that when loyalty prevails, there is more value present in a handshake or a hug than in a signed contract with a disloyal party.

Prayer

"God, help me to be a loyal person. Amen."

Decision

Today I have decided to: _____

_____

_____

_____

_____

14 LOVE

Verse

"And Jonathan had David reaffirm his oath out of love for him, because he loved him as he loved himself." 1 Samuel 20:17 NIV

Thought

Jesus once said, "love your neighbor as yourself" (Mark 12:31). That is a radical idea. This idea suggests that whatever we would do for ourselves, we must be ready and willing to do the same for someone else. Jonathan and David were such good friends that Jonathan was described as loving David as much as he loved himself. If Cain had loved his brother Abel like that, he would never have killed him. If Esau had loved Jacob like that, he would not have deceived him. If we are determined to love others, we will do everything possible to get into a position to help them if needed.

So many people strive for financial success for the sole purpose of securing various things for themselves. However, these people may find that God will bless them with even more if they are willing to share their blessings with others through acts of love.

There are many ways that this may show up in our lives. We may see or do this with our families, close friends or even strangers. A simple act of kindness, a monetary gift or donation, or a favor (big and small). However, a true act of love comes with the intention of not expecting anything in return.

One of the most compelling movies I have ever seen was *John Q*, which featured Denzel Washington who played the role of a father whose son needed a heart transplant. The hospital would not perform the transplant surgery because John's health insurance would not pay for the operation. This desperate father loved his son so much that he was prepared to end his own life to make his heart available for his son. He loved his son more than he loved himself.

John Q was literally ready and willing to sacrifice himself because he loved his son that much. Although Jonathan's love for David was not as drastic, he was taking a huge risk because his father hated David and planned to kill him. True love is not dependent on others' permission and it is willing to take real risk without anything in return. Real love is when we desire for others to have what we also desire for ourselves.

Prayer

"God, help me to love others as much as I love myself. Amen."

Decision

Today I have decided to: _____

_____

_____

_____

_____

15 LEADERSHIP

Verse

"All those who were in distress or in debt or discontented gathered around him, and he became their commander. About four hundred men were with him." 1 Samuel 22:2 NIV

Thought

There is a level of integrity and loyalty that is possessed by people of meager means that seems to be less prevalent among people that are well to do. I have found great joy in my relationships with many people that are struggling themselves, but despite their personal challenges, they are committed to making things better for others. Apparently, David discovered the same to be true. When he needed real help, those that came to his aid to fight alongside him were those in distress, in debt and discontented. Today we might describe them as being marginalized.

I have found that these are the very people that populate the ranks of great causes and great movements. These are the types of foot soldiers that marched and went to jail with Martin Luther King, Jr.; these are the types of people that enlisted in the United States military after the terrorist attacks of September 11, 2001; and these are the types of people who attend our churches Sunday after Sunday supporting the religious traditions of our communities. When leaders receive the loyal support of selfless people, they must reciprocate as selfless leaders.

That means that if you should decide to follow and support a leader – church leader, political leader, or business leader – make sure they are as committed to you as you are to them. Too often, charismatic leaders attract the people that can least afford to be used and disappointed; and too often, that is exactly what happens. If you continue reading this part of David's story, you will find that David was as committed to the welfare of his men as they were committed to David's success.

These men are also a reminder that we need not wait until everything in our lives is wonderful to commit to a cause. In fact, our future opportunities could very well become visible and available to us through our involvement with some project or organization that needs our help. Many of my employees started out as volunteers and wound up having full-time jobs working with me. You may be distressed, in debt, or discontented, but look up and see an opportunity to use your skills to aid a cause, and the blessing could very well end up being yours.

Prayer

"God, plant me somewhere that I can use my gifts even while I wait for my breakthrough. Amen."

Decision

Today I have decided to: _____

_____

_____

_____

_____

16 WEALTH

Verse

"Now Samuel died, and all Israel assembled and mourned for him; and they buried him at his home in Ramah. Then David moved down into the Desert of Paran. A certain man in Maon, who had property there at Carmel, was very wealthy. He had a thousand goats and three thousand sheep, which he was shearing in Carmel. His name was Nabal and his wife's name was Abigail. She was an intelligent and beautiful woman, but her husband was surly and mean in his dealings—he was a Calebite."
1 Samuel 25:1-3 NIV

Thought

Nabal was described as a very wealthy man. His net assets were revealed to have included one thousand goats and three thousand sheep. By all measurements, Nabal was successful and a part of the upper class. He also had an intelligent, beautiful wife, Abigail. If that were the end of Nabal's resume, we could call him the envy of us all. After all, we celebrate that kind of success.

However, financial wealth alone should not determine whether or not someone is successful. I was once told by a prosecutor that the number one crime in the wealthiest county of a certain state was the crime of incest. Mansions dominate the landscape of this area, but behind closed doors there was a persistent problem of illegality and immorality. That reminded me that character would *always* be more important than cash, and people are more important than profits.

The writer also describes Nabal as surly and mean. Surly means bad tempered. Even with all of his money and assets, Nabal didn't understand that his lifestyle and his legacy would be undermined by his temperament and his personality. It was his personality that caused his men to feel that it was appropriate for them to mistreat David's men. When David sent his men to ask Nabal's men for help, they responded with the kind of meanness that they probably learned from their leader; despite the fact that David and his men had previously protected Nabal and his property. Nabal's wife, Abigail, was so embarrassed by their behavior that she secretly gathered supplies and delivered them to David with an apology.

Nabal ended up dying a premature death and his beautiful, intelligent wife ended up becoming David's wife. God forbid that wealth and fortune ever become substitutes for being a good person who treats others nicely.

Prayer

"God, I pray that you will help me remain a good person when I achieve success. Amen."

Decision

Today I have decided to: _____

_____

_____

_____

_____

VALUE

Verse

"Who will listen to what you say? The share of the man who stayed with the supplies is to be the same as that of him who went down to the battle. All will share alike." I Samuel 30:24 NIV

Thought

When I was thirteen years old, and honestly too small to be playing football, my friends convinced me to join the team. I was determined to play. I attended practice regularly and wore my uniform to the games, but I rarely got a chance to play in an actual game. I begged my parents not to attend any of the games because I didn't want them to watch me sit on the bench the entire time. Once, I actually rolled in the dirt after a game to get my uniform dirty and make it look like I had played that day.

When I became a parent and my sons played basketball, I took pride in attending all of their games from AAU through high school. One son even played college basketball and I attended all of those games as well. I must admit that it was easy for me to do so since my sons actually played in every game. I always admired those parents that attended games as often as my wife and I attended without having a chance to see their children play in the game. I would silently confess that I wasn't sure I could travel to game after game if my kid were likely to sit on the bench the entire game. A few parents were quite angry and resentful that their kids were not getting many chances to play and I sympathized with them.

When I was thirteen, I didn't understand the value of being on the team if I never played in a game. That is what the "evil men and troublemakers" in 1 Samuel 30:22 also failed to understand. David and most of his men had gone out to a battle and they were able to capture all of the flocks and herds of their enemy. Some of the men, however, did not fight, as they stayed behind to protect David's camp. After the battle, David decided that the men that stayed behind played as valuable a role as the men that fought. Therefore, the decision was that all would share equally in the distribution of their winnings.

We often fail to see the value in our own work and in the work of others if it does not seem to have direct impact. I had to learn that on a team, the members that come to practice are the ones that help the starters prepare for the games. Similarly, in a business, the people that clean the offices are performing as valuable a role as those that work in the office. The people that make the products are just as valuable as the ones that sell the products. And in the end, every member of a winning team gets a trophy when the team wins a championship. That is because everyone has value whether their role is in public view or behind the scenes.

Prayer

"God, help me to always see value in my work and the work of others. Amen."

Decision

Today I have decided to: _____

_____

_____

_____

_____

TRAGEDY

Verse

"Saul said to his armor-bearer, 'Draw your sword and run me through, or these uncircumcised fellows will come and run me through and abuse me.'" 1 Samuel 31:4 NIV

Thought

King Saul saw the end of his life and decided that he wanted to make his exit on his own terms. At first glance, this may seem like the greatest tragedy one can experience, and I would not disagree. Choosing to end one's life is an irreversible decision, and we would be surprised if we knew how many people actually give suicide at least one thought during their lifetime.

King Saul was not actually choosing to die. He considered the circumstances that he was facing and there was very little, if any chance, that he could escape or survive. In his mind, tragedy was unavoidable, and he decided to take control. It would be hard to disagree with Saul. He was in the throes of an intense battle. His sons had been killed, he was surrounded by the enemy (Philistines) and he had been seriously wounded. After his bodyguard refused to honor his request, he fell on his own sword.

Most people that give up, however, are not facing such insurmountable circumstances. It can feel as though there is no way out when we are drowning in debt or when our means of income have disappeared. That is one of the seasons in life when we feel like giving up on life itself. But unlike Saul, there is always a way out of financial difficulty no matter the severity.

Saul was facing certain death at the hands of his enemies. Our lenders, creditors and bill collectors are not going to kill us! They may talk and act like they are going to end our lives, but that is their bark and not their bite. When we give up due to financial struggles, or we self-medicate with alcohol and drugs to relieve the pain of financial stress, we are responding as if we are in King Saul's situation. There are always options for financial difficulties, so don't give up! Giving up when you still have options is the *real* tragedy!

There are organizations that help individuals and families to repair their credit. There are companies that can consolidate your debt and turn multiple payments into one affordable payment. There are opportunities to reduce your interest rate and monthly payments. There are alternative plans for your ongoing bills that can save you money. There are ways to increase your income by doing tasks you may have never thought you could be paid to do. There are scholarships available for students.

There are government programs that provide assistance. Do your research. Google search terms that connect you to financial resources for people in your circumstance.

There is a strategy for you, so please don't give up. You can avoid tragedy if you don't give up. The enemy does not have the power to destroy you "...*because the one who is in you is **greater** than the one who is in the world*» (1 John 4:4).

Prayer

"God, give me the strength to never give up. Amen."

Decision

Today I have decided to: _____

_____

_____

_____

_____

PERSEVERANCE

Verse

"How the mighty have fallen! The weapons of war have perished!" 2 Samuel 1:27 NIV

Thought

The events surrounding us can seem overwhelming and insurmountable. When I heard older folks describe the time of World War II, it was hard to believe the kinds of things they had to do. I would almost have nightmares imagining that we might have blackouts as they did – days when all lights would have to be darkened in our houses just in case enemy planes flew overhead. I remember actually seeing bomb shelters that some families had built in the rear of their homes. These were underground facilities to which they would retreat in the event of an attack. Unimaginable! Yet they persevered.

The global pandemic that caused every nation on the planet to practice social distancing, sheltering in place and wearing face masks seemed to be an endless reality. Life as we knew it changed forever after losing more people to COVID-19 than most wars. I imagine that is what life was like during the time of David and Saul when they were warring with the Philistines. There were battles seemingly everywhere, all the time. We read about those times quite casually as if they are fiction, but when one lives in the midst of one of these realities, it is undeniable.

Sometimes, we can be so focused on the events around us that we fail to understand, manage, and plan our own finances. We can become so stuck in observing political fights, national news, and world events that we lose sight of basic personal things like managing our budget, controlling our spending, saving for emergencies, and looking for ways to increase our income.

During the COVID-19 pandemic, many people took online courses to learn new skills that they could use after the pandemic was over. They were preparing for what was to come as they persevered through the unknown.

We sing a song in our church, *"Trouble Don't Last Always"*, by Reverend Timothy Wright, that is a true sentiment for all things we endure in this life. There will come a time when the weapons of war will perish, and the troubles will cease. What will you be prepared to do when that day comes?

Prayer

"God, help me to focus on me and persevere while I also observe what is happening in the world around me. Amen."

Decision

Today I have decided to: _____

_____

_____

_____

_____

20 REVERSAL

Verse

"Then the men of Judah came to Hebron, and there they anointed David king over the tribe of Judah." 2 Samuel 2:4 NIV

Thought

There are a handful of events that have captured the attention of the entire world. In fact, most of the nations of the world exist only paying attention to what's going on in their own nation, and few people are able to identify the name and location of most of the world's countries. Most of us do well to remember the names of the seven continents and can manage a few key countries within each, but every generation remembers a few key countries because of some significant, historic event that is etched in their memories. Such an event is the ascendance of Mr. Nelson Mandela, who became the President of the Republic of South Africa in 1994.

His story is so phenomenal that it has propelled South Africa into that small collection of nations that has global recognition and notoriety. Like Caesar, Alexander, Napoleon, George Washington, Hitler, Mao and Kennedy,

Mandela's name resonates with timeless significance and universal wonder. But unlike any other name, Mandela's name represents the most unlikely occurrence of reversal in the history of the world.

Here was a man who was expected to spend the rest of his life in jail. His crime was to oppose the South African government that had implemented a system of apartheid that allowed the white minority of that country to deny the black majority their right to social, political and economic freedom. In South Africa, a black person would have to show a pass if they were on the streets of their community after a certain hour. The apartheid was implemented by an authoritarian political culture based on *baasskap (or* white supremacy), which ensured that South Africa was dominated politically, socially, and economically by the nation's minority white population. According to this system of social separation, white citizens had the highest status, followed by Asians and coloreds (mixed race), and then black Africans. Nelson Mandela was a black African.

Mandela was an attorney that led the African National Congress (ANC) which was the opposition party to the National Party that took power and instituted apartheid in 1948. He was imprisoned for twenty-seven years and labeled as a terrorist even by the United States of America. However, in 1991, just one year after being released from prison, Mr. Mandela became the president of South Africa! This was a stunning political and personal reversal.

When David became King of Judah, he too experienced a reversal. Although he had been anointed by the prophet Samuel to be the next king, King Saul did everything in his power to prevent that from happening; but God protected David and his destiny could not be stopped.

We believe in the God of reversals, and the same God that changed the circumstances of David and Mandela can transform your situation completely. Faith says it is possible even when all of the facts say it is not.

Prayer

"God, increase my faith. Amen."

Decision

Today I have decided to: _____

_____

_____

_____

_____

HELP

Verse

"Now Hiram king of Tyre sent envoys to David, along with cedar logs and carpenters and stonemasons, and they built a palace for David."
2 Samuel 5:11 NIV

Thought

After David became King of Israel, he led his people to attack the Jebusites who were the occupants of the place that he would claim as The City of David, now known as Jerusalem. Although this is the very place that is the focus of debate, contention and periodic physical conflict today, at that time, David and his people were supported and befriended by Hiram, a neighboring king. I am sure David realized that he couldn't fight every nation in the region, and he must have appreciated the help of Hiram, who became his ally.

You do not need to be the ruler of a nation or the head of a large organization to realize that there comes a time when help is needed. There are agencies in every community whose sole purpose is to help those in need. There are government resources available to support people that are experiencing challenges of almost any kind. Perhaps you have decided to change careers; or maybe you have always wanted to start a new business; or you may have a couple of years of college and feel like now is the time to go back and finish school. Whatever our circumstance, we may find ourselves seeking and accepting assistance from a reliable or friendly source.

It is often tempting to try and do things alone because we don't know whom to trust. We may also be embarrassed due to the sensitive nature of our situation, or we may just be too stubborn and prideful to accept help. But accepting help from others is not a sign of weakness or failure. It is quite the opposite. Accepting support and help is a mature and strategic thing to do. Of course, we do have to vet the assistance that is being offered. There are so many scams that come disguised as assistance and that can actually make our lives worse; but there may very well be a Hiram or two in our lives that are willing to invest in us and do for us things that we cannot do for ourselves.

I have received so much valuable help from the most unlikely sources, and I have learned that the best help comes from people that don't need anything from me and don't want anything in return. These folks just want to help me because they believe in me and what I am attempting to do in my life and work. Apparently, that was Hiram's motive, and he helped David without expecting anything in return. David perceived Hiram's help as having come from God to affirm his position as King of Israel.

Sometimes God uses people to represent his love for us, and God uses those very people to deliver his assistance.

Prayer

"God, please help me to recognize when I need help from others and make me receptive to help from the right people. Amen."

Decision

Today I have decided to: _____

_____

_____

_____

_____

22 ORDER

Verse

*"And I will provide a place for my people Israel
and will plant them so that they can have a
home of their own and no longer be disturbed.
Wicked people will not oppress them anymore,
as they did at the beginning and have done
ever since the time I appointed leaders over my
people Israel. I will also give you rest from all your
enemies. The LORD declares to you that the LORD
himself will establish a house for you: When your
days are over and you rest with your ancestors, I
will raise up your offspring to succeed you, your
own flesh and blood, and I will establish his
kingdom. He is the one who will build a house for
my Name, and I will establish the throne of his
kingdom forever."* 2 Samuel 7:10-13 NIV

Thought

I believe the easiest way for people to understand God is
by observing the behavior of Christians and therefore the
Church. I believe Christianity – organized religion as it

is called – should make a tangible difference in the lives of Christians. Modern Christianity, especially in western societies, has put so much emphasis on building religious institutions that much of the gospel of Jesus has been distorted and even abused. This is why I place so much emphasis on the way Christians handles our finances and provide for our families. There are several good reasons to maintain this focus.

In Proverbs we learn that, "a good person leaves an inheritance for their children's children..." (Proverbs 13:22). Previous generations seemed to have been committed to the idea that their children and grandchildren should be their priorities. They found ways to save money, invest in real estate and buy life insurance. They believed in education because they believed that their offspring would have more opportunities if they did well in school. They were passionate about moral values and pursued moral excellence as a strategic response to discrimination and injustice. When my generation was growing up, we heard daily messages concerning what kind of behavior, skills and strategies we would need to be successful in the world. This was a key part of our culture.

The Federal Reserve recently reported that 39% of Americans don't have enough money on hand to cover a $400 emergency. Of course, there are many factors that make the ability to save money quite complicated, but one main factor is that in our consumer culture, saving money is not as valued a practice as spending money. The not-for-profit organizations that advocate saving for emergencies and retirement are overpowered by the massive messaging for purchasing and promotions for easy access to credit. Saving is no longer a priority – it is an after-thought at best.

God promised David that he would establish a house for him even before there was a house built for God. David wanted to build the temple to honor and celebrate the God who had provided for him and his people. God made it his divine priority to build a house for David and left the responsibility of building God's house to David's son. This decision would protect David from leaving a legacy for religious practice yet no inheritance for his children.

Perhaps we should accept God's process and help our members own their own houses the way God promised to make sure David had his own house. Leaders today should encourage their followers to build their own homes instead of helping them build gigantic churches. If churches prosper while the people that support the churches are struggling, the leaders probably missed this passage. Every Christian has the right to have a place of their own and the church should help them achieve it.

Prayer

"God, help me to live below my means so I can save money. Amen."

Decision

Today I have decided to: _____

_____

_____

_____

23 LEGACY

Verse

"The king asked, 'Is there no one still alive from the house of Saul to whom I can show God's kindness?' Ziba answered the king, 'There is still a son of Jonathan; he is lame in both feet.'"
2 Samuel 9:3 NIV

Thought

This is one of the great passages of scripture in the Bible. David and Jonathon, Saul's son, were best friends. King Saul was jealous of David and tried to kill him. By this time in the story, both Jonathon and Saul were dead, and David succeeded Saul as the second King of Israel. Typically, in ancient times, a new king would either exile or kill the family of the previous king when there had been animosity between them, but rather than seek to destroy Saul's family, David sought to show kindness to anyone in his lineage. His servant, Ziba, informed David that his friend, Jonathon, had a son who was still alive. His name was Mephibosheth. David sent for his friend's son and made a seat for him at his table and a place for him in his kingdom.

I once asked a Ghanaian king the meaning of the word tribe. As a westerner, that word generally implied something barbaric and therefore negative. This African King offered a much different perspective. The kingdom that he rules has a history that dates back to the fourteenth century. His one-word answer to the question of the meaning of tribe was profound: *legacy*.

I thought about David when I heard that answer. Think of all of the things David is remembered for. He was the shepherd turned child warrior who killed the giant enemy, Goliath; he was the popular young soldier who was celebrated for killing tens of thousands; he led God's people in numerous battles against enemy nations; he wrote most of the Psalms. Now, added to this list of achievements, we learn that he adopted the grandson of the man who tried to kill him.

That young man, Mephibosheth – someone who suffered from an inability to walk – inherited a relationship that he could not have ever imagined. He had been living in a slum for disabled people – a place called Lodebar, but God blessed him to become a beneficiary of someone else's prosperity.

David's kindness is so exemplary. That is why we should want to prosper; that should be our ultimate goal for achieving wealth and having means. The more we have and achieve, the more we can leave to others as an inheritance.

Prayer

"God, help me prosper so I can leave an inheritance and a legacy for my children and others' children. Amen."

Decision

Today I have decided to: _____

_____

_____

_____

_____

Verse

*"After the time of mourning was over, David
had her brought to his house, and she became
his wife and bore him a son. But the thing
David had done displeased the Lord."*
2 Samuel 11:27 NIV

Thought

Often, people with power have rights and privileges that
common people do not have. David was accustomed
to royal power, royal treatment and royal benefits.
The more someone is exposed to being in a position of
power, the more it is possible to believe that he or she is
excluded from morality. This is what happened to King
David.

Financial success and the attainment of wealth can become
so intoxicating that someone can become delusional. The
key delusion is that success grants a person exemption
from being morally responsible and socially aware,
leaving them to forget qualities such as justice, compassion
and empathy. For instance, capitalism is not inherently

oppressive, but when corporations' main focus becomes their financial return, they abandon the core values of a just society. Many humans have suffered as a result of corporations dumping toxic waste in areas populated by low-income citizens whose exposure to this waste has caused poor health in families for generations. This type of institutional immorality is a result of individuals believing that morality is defined by what one can get away with.

King David literally got away with murder. His desire for Bathsheba motivated him to use his power to assign her husband, Uriah, to a military project that was sure to send him to his death. Because of his power, he had the right to do it without having to consider whether or not the decision was right or wrong. In fact, because of his position as king, this action was automatically considered to be right. *"But the thing David had done displeased the Lord"* (2 Samuel 11:27).

Just because something is legal does not make it right. Slavery was legal; Segregation was legal; and for those in power, the laws that facilitated such practices were right. This was moral exclusivity - morality without social justice. That is why morality must be determined by what pleases God rather than what pleases people.

Prayer

"God, help me to always seek to do what pleases you. Amen."

Decision

Today I have decided to: _____

_____

_____

_____

_____

ACCOUNTABILITY

Verse

"Then Nathan said to David, 'You are the man! This is what the Lord, the God of Israel, says: 'I anointed you king over Israel, and I delivered you from the hand of Saul'". 2 Samuel 12:7 NIV

Thought

King David sent Uriah into battle to certain death because he wanted his wife, Bathsheba, for himself. Even if someone in his kingdom or on his leadership team knew his motives, it would have been highly unlikely that anyone would challenge his decision or his action. That is an unfortunate truth about people in power. They often surround themselves with yes-people who function as cheerleaders instead of true advisors. Many leaders have been poorly served by such flatterers whose goals are generally to gain personal favor rather than to contribute to the success and mission of the person in power.

Nathan was a prophet and was committed to telling David the truth about his behavior even if it could have cost him his relationship with the king. He understood the risk he was taking by challenging David about what he had done to Uriah. Guided by God, Nathan wisely told David a story that caused David to actually identify his own sinful deed.

Perhaps more people could be encouraged to use such an approach when holding people accountable to righteous behavior. You do not need to be famous or in a position of power to need someone like Nathan to keep you accountable. Everyone can use someone in their lives who will tell them the truth when they fall short of communicating with others, treating people fairly, or generally conducting themselves in a wholesome and respectable manner.

We have all heard of the social term, designated driver, where friends who are planning to consume alcohol designate one friend to monitor and minimize the consumption amongst the group, as well as remain sober in order to drive others home after the event. Perhaps we need a system of designated drivers for behavioral critique; where someone in a circle of associates is given permission to honestly share with others an assessment of behaviors that can impact the quality of their group or interpersonal interaction. Some groups establish accountability partners where people have permission to hold each other accountable to established principles and goals. This has worked well in our dfree® movement where people hold one another accountable to debt reduction, spending habits and savings goals. It has also encouraged people to speak honestly to one another about other compulsive behaviors, like overeating, gambling, cursing, etc.

King David ultimately paid a price for his murderous deed. Perhaps if he had consulted with Nathan before he acted, he would have made a better decision. Find someone that will hold you accountable so that you can avoid making permanent decisions for temporary gain.

Prayer

"God, help me find an accountability partner who will help me be a better person. Amen."

Decision

Today I have decided to: _____

_____

_____

_____

_____

CONSEQUENCES

Verse

"Absalom ordered his men, 'Listen! When Amnon is in high spirits from drinking wine and I say to you, 'Strike Amnon down,' then kill him. Don't be afraid. Haven't I given you this order? Be strong and brave.'" 2 Samuel 13:28 NIV

Thought

My sixth-grade teacher thought I would never complete high school. However, I did graduate from high school, and as senior class president, gave the speech at my graduation. My high school career coincided with the civil rights movement, because of this, the black students in my school were exposed to and involved in plenty of social activism. We were the minority in the student body, consisting of only 24% of the total enrollment. We organized a black student union to make sure black students were aware of the resources and opportunities that the school had to offer. We boycotted school when the school administration attempted to deny us the right to form a black student union; and we had numerous events to promote black pride and black student rights.

Although none of our protests were met with stiff disciplinary responses from our school administrators, many protests and demonstrations in other parts of the country resulted in the activists receiving penalties for their acts of civil and institutional disobedience. I always wondered how my friends and I would have responded if we had been penalized for our activities. My thoughts on the subject were presented as a part of my graduation speech where I stated that: *people should be willing to accept the consequences of their actions*. I was being directly critical of people that violated various rules in support of their beliefs and then asked for forgiveness to avoid the penalty that resulted from their actions. Even at that young age, I believed that we should expect and accept consequences for our decisions and our behavior.

That is why I don't think Amnon should have been surprised by Absalom's orders. His infraction was much more serious than any student protest. Amnon physically forced himself on his and Absalom's sister, Tamar, and raped her. Absalom's response would certainly be considered extreme, but Amnon had to know that he would pay for what he did.

Every decision we make comes with consequences. Every financial choice we make has consequences. Life is a series of cause-and-effects and it is naïve to believe we can avoid the outcomes caused by our decisions. Therefore, it would benefit us to think very carefully before we act and to choose wisely before we make a move.

Prayer

"God, show me the consequences of my decisions. Amen."

Decision

Today I have decided to: _____

_____

_____

_____

_____

27 GOODWILL

Verse

"Then the king said to Ziba, 'All that belonged to Mephibosheth is now yours.' 'I humbly bow,' Ziba said. 'May I find favor in your eyes, my lord the king.'" 2 Samuel 16:4 NIV

Thought

I serve on the board of a major financial institution. By major, I mean the institution is worth billions of dollars and is connected to other institutions that are worth more than a trillion dollars collectively. This company is so unique and exclusive that when I received the call to serve on the board, I had never even heard of it and had to research to find out about it. The person who arranged for me to be appointed to that board did not know me very well, had rarely interacted with me, and certainly did not owe me anything. Apparently, he was familiar enough with me and my work and admired what he knew. Without knowing that one of my goals was to serve as a director on corporate boards, he submitted my name to the appointing authority, and I became a corporate director for the second time in my life. That directorship opened doors for five more positions on corporate boards, and I now teach an online course called, *"How to Become a Corporate Director."*

I did absolutely nothing to position myself for that opportunity. The fact that I was offered access to something that I didn't work to achieve, did not position myself to receive, and didn't even know existed is how I define favor. I learned that from Ziba, a servant who had worked for King Saul. King David initially showed kindness to Mephibosheth because of his love for his father, Jonathan. He also showed kindness to the servant, Ziba, even though his master, Mephibosheth, was disloyal to David. This was almost unthinkable, as David could - and perhaps should - have considered Ziba disloyal too. Even Ziba was surprised and referred to this as favor.

Some may consider this kind of occurrence as luck. However, luck is mere coincidence. Favor, on the other hand, requires that someone is put in a position to receive benefits without regard for their qualifications or eligibility. In other words, one cannot earn or win favor. It is completely unpredictable and controlled by the person that has the power to grant it.

That is what we receive from God every day – *favor*. If God gave us what we deserved, it would be punishment for the bad thoughts, bad words, bad choices and bad actions that we commit. However, God extends grace to us – grace being undeserved favor – and blesses us with so much more than we deserve. Therefore, we should never become so preoccupied with the blessings that we have yet to receive that we cannot recognize the favor of God and what we have received already.

Prayer

"God, help me to remain aware of and grateful for your favor. Amen."

Decision

Today I have decided to: _____

_____

_____

_____

_____

Verse

"The king was shaken. He went up to the room over the gateway and wept. As he went, he said: 'O my son Absalom! My son, my son Absalom! If only I had died instead of you - O Absalom, my son, my son!'" 2 Samuel 18:33 NIV

Thought

One of the many reasons I had such respect for both of my grandmothers is because of the way they each handled the deaths of their children. My maternal grandmother, Mary Pinkard, was predeceased by two of her sons. My paternal grandmother, Carrie Soaries, was predeceased by one daughter and two sons, including my dad. I watched both of them as they showed unimaginable strength while they lowered the people who had come out of their wombs into the ground.

The images of my grandmothers losing their children became intensely personal for me when I became a father. Just the thought of having to bury one of my sons is perhaps the most intimidating and frightening thought I can imagine. David was the king and his son

Absalom had been rebellious against him, but when David received the news that his son was dead, he was inconsolable. This was what could easily be called, calamity, for David.

A calamity is when something happens that is a disaster. Losing anyone you love is a personal disaster, but death is not the only way calamity can strike a family. In fact, the calamities that we are most likely to experience are finance related. When a loved one spends weeks in hospital and the health insurance provider only covers a small percentage of the bill, that can be a calamity. When you have one hundred thousand dollars in student loans and your salary is $35,000 a year, that can be a calamity. If you went through a divorce and now are responsible for half of the bills that were accrued during the marriage, that can be a calamity.

I am not sure David could have done much to avoid his calamity because Absalom had an agenda and thought he knew what was best in most matters. However, there are ways we can prepare and minimize the likelihood of financial matters turning into calamities. We can control our spending and make our needs take precedence over our wants. We can live within our means and have the discipline to only spend what we really have. We can pay our bills on time and spare ourselves the high cost of late fees and other penalties. We can check our credit reports and guard against identity theft. We can invest in insurances that protect us in the event of accidents and incidents that attack our assets or our ability to earn an income. Additionally, we can save for emergencies and towards retirement.

In other words, we can prepare ourselves in order to avoid financial calamity. We can model responsible financial living for those around us, especially our children whose relationships with money will be shaped by our behavior and instruction.

Prayer

"God, help me do whatever I can to avoid calamity. Amen."

Decision

Today I have decided to: _____

_____

_____

_____

_____

CONFUSION

Verse

"You love those who hate you and hate those who love you." 2 Samuel 19:6 NIV

Thought

In 2008 there was an event that impaired the entire global economy. Financial institutions that were considered to be unshakeable, went out of business; millions of foreclosures forced people out of their homes; and the unemployment rate skyrocketed. An expert in finance described the cause for our crisis as "irrational exuberance." What he meant was that the people that make investment decisions became consumed by an attraction to strategies that produced short term successes but that were destined to fail in the long run.

Institutional investors are very smart people who are supported by teams of analysts and researchers feeding them information on which they base their investment decisions. These investors thrive on the process of their financial decisions that bring the companies they work for money. What they failed to realize was that their financial risks would cause Wall Street to come to a screeching halt. Some of the smartest people in finance seemed to be confused because they had become emotionally attached to the investment instruments that ended up destroying them along with the rest of us.

It is damaging to cling to things that actually do us harm. This idea of loving someone or something that hates you sounded illogical when David's men said it to him. They were confused as to how David could grieve over a son who outwardly despised him, and forget his people who had been loyal to him. David's men thought he was confused. How could he love someone who hated him?

In our humanness, it is easy to gravitate towards things that aren't good for us. Take tobacco for example. Since 1969 cigarette companies have been required to place a message on their packaging: **WARNING: THE SURGEON GENERAL HAS DETERMINED THAT CIGARETTE SMOKING IS DANGEROUS TO YOUR HEALTH. Yet despite this warning and the ever-increasing prices, people continue to use cigarettes to relax. They've actually fallen in love with something that can kill them!**

We seem to have an attraction to self-destructive decisions. Unfortunately, sophisticated advertising campaigns use mass marketing techniques to lure us into developing strong attractions to less than healthy choices. This may be a much more lethal reality for us than the tragedy that David experienced.

At its core, materialism is the state of falling in love with material things. People kill one another over things. Crimes are committed in an effort to obtain more things. Relationships are destroyed because of disputes over things. That is why John stated, "*Do not love the world or anything in the world*" (1 John 3:15 NIV).

At least David was not grieving over the loss of material things. He was displaying love for his son despite his son's disrespect and insurrection. His men may have thought David was confused, but the king had a right to grieve over the death of his son. The real tragedy and confusion are when we become attached to inanimate objects and love them so much that we cannot separate ourselves from them even when they prove to be harmful. That is when we have allowed the good to be confused with the bad, and that confusion can destroy us.

Prayer

"God, please keep me from being confused. Amen."

Decision

Today I have decided to: _____

_____

_____

_____

_____

GOLIATH

Verse

"In another battle with the Philistines at Gob, Elhanan son of Jair the Bethlehemite killed the brother of Goliath the Gittite, who had a spear with a shaft like a weaver's rod."
2 Samuel 21:19 NIV

Thought

It was good news to the Israelites when a young man named David defeated the giant adversary, Goliath. Although David's victory ultimately infuriated King Saul, the people celebrated their champion. Whenever anyone faces and defeats an enemy or obstacle as significant as Goliath, it is cause for celebration.

In many ways, Goliath is a metaphor representing the many challenges that come in life. The lesson that the David-Goliath encounter offers us people of faith, is the confidence that our obstacles can be defeated. I have learned to name my challenges, my problems and my obstacles, Goliath, because that reminds me that I can overcome them.

Goliath was over nine feet tall, well-armed and had a bodyguard. Soldiers were afraid of Goliath and not one of them would accept his challenge to fight. Some problems are legitimately big enough to be intimidating even to the best among us. However, David's use of an unconventional weapon brought a troublesome opponent to his knees and enabled the Israelites to put another battle in the win column. With only a slingshot and five smooth stones, the young boy claimed victory and brought relief to the entire nation. But Goliath had a family, including a brother who was as intimidating as Goliath himself. When Goliath's brother appeared with the Philistines in a battle against Israel, David may have said to himself, "here we go again."

Life has a way of reminding us that as long as we live, we will face Goliaths, and that after we defeat Goliath, we will have to confront his brother. While many of us thought that we had defeated the Goliath of segregation and racial injustice, we now realize that Goliath had family – siblings, children, nieces, nephews and cousins. That simply means we must always remain vigilant, alert and prepared to fight new battles and defeat new enemies. In order to do that, we must stay fit physically, mentally, spiritually *and* financially. The same strength that David used to kill Goliath was still available for facing his brother; and the same God that gave us the power to defeat the enemies of injustice and freedom is available to help us now. We must be sure to depend on that power and recognize the need to be ready for Goliath's family.

Prayer

"God, give me the strength to keep fighting. Amen."

Decision

Today I have decided to: _____

_____

_____

_____

_____

BARGAINING

Verse

*"'Your Majesty, Araunah gives all this to the king.'
Araunah also said to him, 'May the Lord your
God accept you.' But the king replied to Araunah,
'No, I insist on paying you for it. I will not sacrifice
to the Lord my God burnt offerings that cost me
nothing.'"* 2 Samuel 24:23-24 NIV

Thought

The king needed a place to build an altar for a religious
service of sacrifice. Araunah owned the threshing floor on
Mount Moriah that was appropriate for the purpose. This
is a classic formation of what economists call, supply and
demand. Araunah had the supply, a threshing floor, and
David had the demand – a need for a place to build an
altar. David was what could be called a motivated buyer
because there was a plague in the land caused by his sin
(we are not sure which specific sin), killing thousands of
people.

Whenever someone has a need to buy something that
exceeds the need of the seller, an inflated transaction is
likely to occur, especially if the product cannot be easily

purchased elsewhere. The dynamics of this encounter are intriguing because although Araunah was in a position of advantage, he didn't see it as an opportunity to maximize his profit. Instead, he chose to serve the king and thus the nation by offering to donate his threshing floor.

This offer defies a core principle of capitalism which argues that market forces should always profit. Araunah possessed values that led him to put the principles of loyalty to God and his nation before financial gain. He made an offer that no one required of him. Unfortunately, businesses rarely make these kinds of decisions. Without regulatory standards, many businesses would take advantage of the market and overcharge whenever they wanted. We find this to be true in times of disasters when prices for certain items skyrocket because they are in short supply and high demand. Price gouging is the result of businesses run by people who do not possess an Araunah spirit.

As a result of Araunah's kind offer to donate the threshing floor, King David insisted on paying for it in full. David's offer was not only in response to his need of the product, but also in appreciation for the fact that Araunah did not try to hustle him under the circumstances.

Some people believe that hard knuckle negotiating is the only reasonable approach to doing business. However, sometimes graciousness is rewarded with more than we ever could have expected to receive. It's important to know when to be tough and when to be gracious.

Prayer

"God, show me when to be tough and when to be gracious. Amen."

Decision

Today I have decided to: _____

_____

_____

_____

_____

dfree®
FINANCIAL FREEDOM
MOVEMENT™

www.mydfree.org

ABOUT THE AUTHOR

DeForest B. Soaries, Jr. served as the Senior Pastor of First Baptist Church of Lincoln Gardens (FBCLG) in Somerset, New Jersey from November 1990 to July 2021. His 30 years of pastoral ministry focused on spiritual growth, educational excellence and economic empowerment.

As a pioneer of faith-based community development, Dr. Soaries' impact on First Baptist Church of Lincoln Gardens (FBCLG) and the community was tremendous. In 1992, he founded the Central Jersey Community Development Corporation (CJCDC), a 501(c)(3) non-profit organization that specializes in revitalizing distressed neighborhoods. In 1996, Soaries founded the Harvest of Hope Family Services Network, Inc. (HOH). This organization developed permanent solutions for children in the foster care system.

From 1999 to 2002, Dr. Soaries served as New Jersey's Secretary of State, making him the first African-American male to do so. He also served as the former chairman of the United States Election Assistance Commission, which was established by Congress to implement the "Help America Vote Act" of 2002.

In 2005, Dr. Soaries launched the dfree® Financial Freedom Movement. The dfree® strategy teaches people how to break free from debt as a first step toward financial freedom and it is currently being used across the country by thousands of churches and organizations. dfree® was featured in a 90-minute CNN documentary entitled *Almighty Debt*. He is author of the books "Say Yes to No Debt," "dfree Lifestyle: 12 Steps to Financial Freedom," "Meditations for Financial Freedom - Volumes 1&2," and "Say Yes When Life Says No" (book and workbook).

Dr. Soaries serves as an independent director at three companies: Independence Realty Trust (IRT), Federal Home Loan Bank of New York and Ocwen Financial Corporation. He is also a board member at RWJ Barnabas Health. He teaches an online Master Class "How to Become a Corporate Director" and mentors aspiring corporate directors.

Dr. Soaries earned a Bachelor of Arts Degree from Fordham University, a Master of Divinity Degree from Princeton Theological Seminary, and a Doctor of Ministry Degree from United Theological Seminary. He has been honored with seven honorary doctorate degrees.

Dr. Soaries resides in Monmouth Junction, New Jersey with his wife, Donna, and twin sons.

www.ingramcontent.com/pod-product-compliance
Lightning Source LLC
Chambersburg PA
CBHW060627210326
41520CB00010B/1508